# FINDING JESUS

# FINDING JESUS

## *Living Through Lent with John's Gospel*

GERALD O'COLLINS, S.J.

*Illustrations by*
*William McNichols, S.J.*

PAULIST PRESS · NEW YORK · RAMSEY

Library of Congress
Catalog Card Number:
83-62470


ISBN:
0-8091-2565-X

Published by Paulist Press
545 Island Road
Ramsey, N.J. 07446

Printed and bound in the
United States of America

# CONTENTS

# Foreword

Several years ago I was sharing a platform with a genial rabbi who—apropos of the current state of exegesis, theology and spirituality—complained provocatively to our totally Christian audience: "These days there are no conclusions: there are only methods." My mind jumped at once to John's Gospel and I thought: "If Jesus is our method when we read that text, we will reach some conclusions and they will be spiritually valid."

This book is an invitation to "come and see" (John 1:39)—to experience the Jesus of John's Gospel for ourselves. If we have the courage to make a start and let that experience grow, conclusions will emerge and we will see things which previously have remained below the level of our spiritual consciousness.

At the heart of the Dutch verb "to experience" *(er-varen)* nestles the old verb *varen* which means "to travel by boat." It conjures up visions

1

not only of rowing laboriously or of being pulled along by a horse plodding down the side of a canal, but also of finding a favorable following wind to fill the sails. This little work is written in the hope that Jesus will come to fill our sails and carry us along, just as we find him filling the sails of Andrew, the Samaritan woman and others in John's story.

This Gospel has a strongly experiential and contemplative quality. It hands on what has been over and over again experienced in life and contemplated in prayer—*contemplata tradere,* as the lovely Dominican motto puts it. For any who doubt that experience and contemplation go together, John is the best answer. We can properly describe this Gospel as one long act in which the glory of God is experienced and contemplated in Christ. It begins with the community's witness to their personal experience of the incarnate Word—"We have seen his glory" (1:14)—and draws to a close with Thomas looking at the risen Christ and confessing, "My Lord and my God" (20:28).

In this book I plan to develop and share some themes of Johannine spirituality. For much that I have learned in this area I wish to express my warm thanks to Raymond Brown, Michael J. Buckley, William Dych, George MacRae, Edward Malatesta, Cardinal Carlo Martini, the late Donatien Mollat, C. F. D. Moule, and Peter Steele. I am deeply grateful to them all, although I do not want to make anyone responsible for the precise ways I react to John's text. Unless otherwise noted, all references are to that Gospel. Some of the material in Chapters One and Two has appeared in *America* magazine, and a little of the material in Chapter Five has appeared in *The Way*, a quarterly review of contemporary Christian spirituality published by the English Jesuits. All the material is reprinted with permission.

Finally, this little work is dedicated with love and admiration to James and Jacquelyn McDonald, their son (Mark), daughters (Julia, Maria, Alexandra and Anne), and daughter-in-law (Patricia).

# JESUS THE QUESTIONER

# 1

## *Jesus the Questioner*

I remember a cartoon in which a series of scenes showed a young man moving from excellent health through to his death. On the way he explained: "I thought politics was the answer. But it failed. I thought revolution was the answer. But it failed. I thought religion was the answer. But it failed. I thought survival was the answer. But it failed." In the last scene a voice asked from the grave: "What could be the answer?" The answer might be to look for the right questions.

### I

It has often been said that a wise person is one who pauses *to ask the right questions* rather than rushing on at once to give the "correct" answers. The Bible and John's Gospel, however, imply that it would be more accurate to say that the wise person is one who pauses *to hear and ponder the right questions.*

In the Book of Genesis God soon confronts Adam with a question: "Where are you?" (3:9). Right through the Old Testament God continues to challenge people with utterly basic questions: "What have you been doing? Where are you going? Why have you abandoned me?" In the face of Job's complaints about his sufferings, the divine Questioner does not offer explanations, but speaks out of a whirlwind: "I will question you" (Job 38:3). The climax of that book (38–41) shows God searching Job with a battery of questions about the power, the beauty and the mystery of the created universe. Here one might adapt the opening line of Hopkins' "Wreck of the Deutschland" and entitle these last chapters of Job, "Thou questioning me God."

The Old Testament records various truths, commands, invitations and warnings which God communicated to individuals and through them to the chosen people. But the Scriptures also indicate that at times the word of God took the form of a question. Isaiah, for example, recalls that vision in the temple which brought his prophetic vocation. His mouth was purified, and then he heard "the voice of the Lord" asking, "Whom shall I send, and who will go for us?" (6:8). God could be a questioning God.

It comes then as no surprise that in John the very first words of Jesus are a question: "What are

8

you looking for?" (1:38). The divine Questioner has become flesh to dwell among us.

The other Gospels aim primarily at setting forth various traditions about the human life, ministry, passion, death and resurrection of Jesus Christ. Unlike the Fourth Gospel they do not plan to set out his divinity with dazzling and direct clarity. In Matthew's Gospel the first words of Jesus occur when Satan tempts him to prove his divine sonship: "If you are the Son of God, command these stones to become loaves of bread." Jesus counters the temptation by quoting what Deuteronomy 8:3 says about the deepest source of human life: "Man shall not live by bread alone, but by every word that proceeds from the mouth of God" (Mt 4:3f). In Luke's Gospel the first words of Jesus occur in the same context (4:4). In Mark, however, no details are offered about the temptation by Satan, and Jesus begins to speak by proclaiming the good news: "The time is fulfilled, and the kingdom of God is at hand; repent, and believe in the gospel" (1:15).

Where the earlier Gospels present Jesus as starting with a scriptural quotation (Matthew and Luke) or with a programmatic announcement (Mark), in the Fourth Gospel his opening words are that terribly simple but profound question: "What are you looking for?" The God who says to Adam "Where are you?" and to Job "I will question you" has come among us and slips at once into the divine habit of asking questions.

Before he presents his message, Jesus first

calls us into question. He wants us to examine what our hearts are set on—what we finally hope to discover in life. Each of us has to ask himself or herself: "What am I really looking for?"

In his divine wisdom Jesus leads us first toward the right questions, rather than pressing ahead at once to provide us with all the true answers. Let us begin by hearing and pondering his questions. Then we may hope to find and follow his answers.

"Make us open to your word, Jesus, and always ready to accept your challenge. Let us lay aside our answers, listen steadfastly to your questions, and find in you what we are all ultimately looking for."

## II

One way then of reading through John's Gospel is to note and mull over the questions of Jesus: from "Will you also go away?" (6:67) to "Do you know what I have done to you?" (13:12), from "Have I been with you so long, and yet you do not know me, Philip?" (14:9) to the awesomely direct question "Do you love me?" (21:15ff). Let me take those four questions in turn.

(1) In her *Live or Die* Anne Sexton offers the advice, "Live or die but don't poison everything." As Peter Steele has pointed out to me, most of us "don't poison *everything*," but we can certainly sour and damage things. We can spoil our lives with random acts of cruelty, cowardice and self-

ishness. It is not quite living and it is not quite dying. It is not quite Christian. It is not really facing Jesus' question, "Will you also go away?"

We can stay with Jesus in a half-hearted way that is not truly living his life. We have not gone away from him. Yet we do not fully belong to him. We remain *near him rather than with him.* We neither live fully in his company, nor do we allow our Christian commitment to die completely.

There is a Jewish proverb which goes: "You can't fool me. I'm too stupid." There is a kind of stupidity we need, a kind of slow simplicity in hearing and turning over the words of Jesus. Only *that* stupidity can stop us from being fooled and from fooling ourselves when we face the question, "Will you also go away?"

There is more than one way of leaving Jesus. There are also many ways of not staying with him fully. He will never force our hand. We live with him either freely or not at all. He hopes that his question will be enough. How could anyone who has known him ever leave him?

"Jesus, let me stay with you fully, and not poison things by my half-hearted love. Where else could I go? You have the words of eternal life."

(2) We spend our lives trying to get behind the surface appearances and really understand what we have been through. What was the meaning of all that? Was there even any meaning in all that?

T. S. Eliot's line "We had the experience but

missed the meaning" touches a raw nerve. Is there any point of going on with life, unless we can somehow eventually understand and express what it has all been about?

The opening of John's Gospel calls Jesus Christ the "Logos," the ultimate meaning of all things. That "Logos" is also light and life (1:4). He is then the luminous and life-giving meaning of things. But Jesus will not always offer us instant explanations. It may take a long time for things to fall into place and the meaning of our experiences to emerge. Simon Peter is warned when Jesus comes to wash his feet: "What I am doing you do not know now, but afterwards you will understand" (13:7).

After washing the feet of all the disciples present, Jesus puts that mysterious question which goes beyond the immediate context and must be wrestled with for a lifetime: "Do you know what I have done to you?" The question is a challenge and a comfort.

It is a challenge. I can *think* I know what Jesus has done to me—both the painful troubles he has caused me and the consoling happiness he has brought me. But do I *really* know and appreciate at any depth what he has been doing to me? Can I hope in this life to penetrate and comprehend that mystery of my personal existence in relationship to Jesus?

If the first half of the question is a challenge ("Do *you know* . . ."), the second half ("what *I have done* to you?") offers comfort. What finally counts in our lives is never our success—-not even our finest achievements—but what Jesus does to us and for us. Andrew spends an afternoon with Jesus and goes to tell his brother, "We have found the Messiah" (1:41). But neither Andrew nor anyone else would ever find Jesus, unless he first comes to find them and make them his own.

Short of our union with him beyond death, we will never fully know all that Jesus has been doing to us. But we can always take comfort in the fact that it is he who has been acting on us and for us.

(3) Jesus' question to Philip ("Have I been with you so long, and yet you do not know me?") can be readily transferred to our own spiritual experience. Many of us are painfully aware that, although we have been so long "with Jesus," we hardly know him. Even now he still comes to us almost as one unknown. "Jesus the Stranger" is a title that touches our own story.

However, that question also suggests a pervasive theme in the Fourth Gospel: the invitation *to experience Jesus* in deeper and richer ways. Philip has been so long with Jesus. But has he really experienced him?

In John simple verbs like "know," "have" and "see" dot the pages. Very often we get the fuller point by substituting our contemporary verb "experience." Thus two individuals are invited, "Come and *experience me* for yourselves" (1:39). The people of Samaria tell the woman who has brought them the news about Jesus that she is now redundant: "It is no longer because of your words that we believe, for we have heard for ourselves, and *experienced* that this is indeed the Savior of the world" (4:42). The Gospel itself is written that "you may believe that Jesus is the Christ, the Son of God, and that believing you *may experience life* in his name" (20:31).

One can easily think of other examples where "experience" catches for us now something of the sense of John's "know," "have" and "see." This is part of the deeply experiential flavor of the Fourth Gospel.

One can also add: the use of such *verbs* is part of the *dynamic* quality of this Gospel, which suggests so well the nature of our relationship with Jesus. Of course, all interpersonal relationships can only be dynamic and changing. We live them, and can never store them up and possess them. Even more so, our relationship with Jesus is something which happens over and over again. We spend a lifetime coming to him, seeing him and experiencing him.

John brings this point out very nicely by the fact that in his Gospel he *never uses the noun* "faith" *(pistis)* but always the verb "to believe" *(pisteuein)*. Nearly one hundred times that verb occurs—right up to the climactic invitation to *"believe* that Jesus is Christ, the Son of God," so that *"believing* you may have life in his name." To believe is to maintain a living, changing, dynamic relationship through the Holy Spirit with Jesus Christ who reveals to us his Father.

John's Gospel introduces other verbs to express the act which puts us in an immediate relationship with the person of Jesus. If not quite identical with "to believe," these synonyms are certainly parallel: "to receive" Jesus (5:43f), "to come" to him (6:35), "to hear" and "follow" him (10:27) and so forth. Here again the verbal language is unmistakable and it implies a deep truth. Can we ever dare say, "Now I know Jesus and have faith in him"? We never *are* believers; at best we are only *becoming* believers in him.

(4) At the end of John's Gospel three times Jesus questions Peter, "Do you love me?" At the Last Supper Jesus has told all the disciples, "No longer do I call you servants . . . but I have called you friends" (15:15). Now he asks whether Peter in his turn is or at least wants to be a loving friend.

Back in Chapter 1 Andrew and his companion make their first move toward discipleship by "coming" and "staying" with Jesus (1:38f). By the close of the Gospel it has become clear that Jesus' disciples are not only to be with Jesus and steadily experience his presence. They are also to be his intimate friends. John in fact is the only Gospel writer who uses "friend" *(philos)* and "to love as a friend" *(philein)* to indicate the heart of a disciple's relationship with Jesus.

Jesus does not ask Peter: "Have you a good plan for organizing the missionary campaign of the Church? Will you prove a successful leader?" But very simply Jesus questions him: "Do you love me?" Loving friendship is all that Jesus wants from Peter or any of us. Finally, Jesus will only question us about our love.

15

This brief chapter has sampled ways in which the Fourth Gospel portrays Jesus as the Questioner. His questions, of course, belong naturally in those dialogues which are a feature of this Gospel.

But we should not miss what all this entails. Those questions and those dialogues were only a beginning. They have gone on and will go on till the end of history. The risen Jesus comes to initiate and remain in dialogue with each of us. If the story of all those dialogues were recorded, "the world itself could not contain the books that would have to be written" (21:25).

It has often been noted that at times Jesus reveals himself in John's Gospel through the "I am" statements: "I am the bread of life. I am the good shepherd. I am the light of the world. I am the true vine. I am the way, the truth and the life." These "I am" statements reach their climax with that stunning claim: "Before Abraham was made, I am" (8:58). The reference is obviously to God's self-revelation to Moses: "I am who I am" (Ex 3:14).

The variety and boldness of these "I am" statements encourage me to add a further one: "I am the questioner and the question."

Anyone who accepts Jesus' company knows that sooner or later he will begin raising questions that are not to be put aside. The Word of God become flesh will consistently disclose himself to us as the divine Questioner. His questions may appear to range across different items. But they all eventually come back to one point. The only question that we must ultimately answer concerns the Questioner himself: "Whom are you looking for?" (20:15). Our response will determine whether we truly live or quietly let ourselves poison and damage things.

"Jesus, whom am I looking for? Is it you whom I always seek?"

# ENCOUNTERING JESUS

# 2

## *Encountering Jesus*

In the Book of Revelation the risen Christ declares: "Behold, I stand at the door and knock; if anyone hears my voice and opens the door, I will come in to him and eat with him, and he with me" (3:20). This verse serves to sum up beautifully a special feature of the Fourth Gospel: the personal approach of Jesus to individual men and women. From the first to the last chapter we can read this Gospel in that key—as a series of one-to-one encounters with Jesus. To be sure, he also meets groups or even crowds of people. But much of the story concerns the meetings with individuals: from Andrew in Chapter 1 to Simon Peter in Chapter 21.

Sometimes those individuals bear names like Nicodemus, Martha and Mary Magdalene. Sometimes they are simply called a Samaritan woman, a royal official, a man sick for thirty-eight years, a woman taken in adultery or a man born blind. But in all cases, when we read prayerfully the stories of these encounters, we may easily slip into the "I-have-been-there" feeling. In all these people we can spot representative spiritual problems and needs. It is not difficult to transfer what we read to our own human and Christian experience.

In this chapter I propose to reflect on some of these encounters with Jesus, taking the stories in their own terms as John presents them. Patterns will begin to emerge when we put some questions to our texts. How do these individuals come to meet Jesus? What might they expect from him? How are they changed? How does the outcome go beyond their expectations?

(1) In John 1:35–42 *Andrew* and his unnamed companion meet Jesus because they have been in John the Baptist's company. Then the Baptist "looks at" Jesus as he walks by and says, "Behold, the Lamb of God!" That significant glance and remark are enough to send Andrew and his friend trailing off after Jesus. What precisely do they expect? At this point we are not clearly told. John has directed them toward this stranger as the One who can relieve the terrible suffering of sin. They exit to spend the rest of the day with Jesus.

The Gospel includes no account of what Jesus talks about with the two men. Once they accept the invitation to "come and see" where he is "staying," the dialogue takes place offstage. Their question "Where are you staying?" has moved the alert reader beyond the sheerly superficial matter of Jesus' current address in Bethany to ponder the deeper meaning of his permanent home as Son of God in his Father's "house" (8:35; 14:2. 10; 15:10). As for the two disciples themselves, when Andrew returns from these first hours with Jesus, we see at once how he has been changed. He goes looking for his brother Simon to tell him, "We have found the Messiah." Andrew and his friend have been looking for nothing less and no one less than the Savior, and now they have found him.

Every believer in Jesus can echo Andrew's cry of joy at finding the One who will set us free or rather at being found by him. The search is over and the burden is lifted. No writer has expressed this quest more poignantly than Dostoevski in *The Brothers Karamazov:* "All my life I have been looking for someone like you to come and forgive me."

Finally, the "missionary" impulse in Andrew is unmistakable. He immediately wants to share with others what he has found and tell them of the One whom he has experienced. He exemplifies perfectly the intention expressed by the First Letter of John: "That which we have seen and heard we proclaim also to you, so that you may have fellowship with us; and our fellowship is with the Father and with his Son Jesus Christ" (1:3). The "missionary" desire to share Jesus with others runs through the stories of the encounters in John's Gospel: from the Samaritan woman's "Come and see a man who told me all

23

that I ever did" (4:29) to Mary Magdalene's "I
have seen the Lord" (20:18).

(2) *Nicodemus* (3:1–21) meets Jesus because
he has gone looking for him. Admittedly he
comes "by night." As a Pharisee, a ruler of the
Jews and a teacher of Israel, Nicodemus is someone who has arrived and who is sensitive to his
own reputation and importance. He is afraid of
compromising himself, and so he decides to visit
Jesus under cover of darkness.

What expectations does Nicodemus have? He
has already reached certain conclusions about
Jesus: "Rabbi, we know that you are a teacher
come from God; for no one can do these signs that
you do, unless God is with him." Apparently Nicodemus simply wants reassurance and confir-
mation about Jesus' being a divinely endorsed
teacher.

But what happens in the dialogue suddenly
goes far beyond the limited agenda Nicodemus
has proposed. Jesus abruptly assures him, "Truly,
truly, I say to you, unless one is born again, he
cannot see the kingdom of God." Jesus spells out
this unexpected invitation to enter the kingdom
as entailing new birth through water and the
Spirit.

Is Nicodemus to submit to God's Spirit which
like the unpredictable and invisible wind "blows
where it wills"? Must he become a born-again
Pharisee?

Nicodemus knows what can happen and
what cannot happen. The words "how" and
"can" recur in his three questions to suggest a

limited view of God's power: *"How can* a man be born when he is old? *Can* he enter a second time into his mother's womb and be born? . . . *How can* this be?"* It is frightening to be called when one is "old" to start once again from the beginning. Is it possible to do so?

Nicodemus is a professionally religious man, a rigid man who has life under control but who also has an ill-defined sense of some personal need. He does come to Jesus of his own accord. But for the time being he has only limited trust in the power of the Spirit.

The story of Nicodemus' encounter with Jesus trails off. There is no clearly indicated ending in the test. A change does come over Nicodemus but it comes slowly. It comes precisely in terms of public courage, the very quality Nicodemus has seemingly lacked. First, he defends Jesus' right to a proper hearing (7:50f). Then after the crucifixion he throws in his lot with the faithful disciples and turns up with an enormous quantity of myrrh and aloes (19:39). He sees to it that Jesus is buried like a king. Although he first visited Jesus under cover of darkness, by acting truly he has finally come to the light (3:21).

(3) It looks like an accident that *the Samaritan woman* (4:4–42) meets Jesus. She could have gone to draw water earlier or later in the day. The midday encounter at Jacob's well seems a perfectly chance meeting. But what begins like a random exchange ends very differently.

Unlike the encounter with Nicodemus, it is Jesus this time who takes the initiative and opens the dialogue: "Give me a drink." To begin with, their interchange centers on something which is not only simple and basic, but also an elemental necessity for human beings and their world— water. The first part of the dialogue ends with Jesus' promise: "Whoever drinks of the water that I shall give him will never thirst; the water that I shall give him will become in him a spring of water welling up to eternal life."

When I read that promise, I always think of the fountains in the Villa d'Este outside Rome. The spouts of crystal-fresh water leap into the air and become charged with sunlight. Like those fountains Jesus gives himself away with joy. The Samaritan woman and the rest of us are not asked to search and dig for water, let alone store it in some reservoir. We simply have to cup our hands and drink.

The encounter at high noon abruptly moves on when Jesus says to the woman, "Go, call your husband." Jesus has touched her irregular home situation. She has had five husbands, and is now living with a man who is not her husband. But she does not break off her dialogue with Jesus in embarrassment. Little by little she lets him lead her on, right to the point when he no longer speaks merely of living water but reveals himself as the living Christ.

Once more we see the missionary impulse in a person who has experienced Jesus at such depth. She does not hoard the news but brings it to the people of Sychar. Many are so impressed by the woman's testimony that they come to believe in Jesus. Later others tell her that she is now re-dundant: "It is no longer because of your words that we believe, for we have heard for ourselves, that this is indeed the Savior of the world." They no longer need the woman's witness to her own experience. They have experienced Jesus for themselves, and they call him by a title we find nowhere else in the New Testament: "the Savior of the world."

If Nicodemus is a slow learner, the sinful Samaritan woman is quite the opposite. This might seem all the more surprising in someone who is no young teenager but a grown woman with a steady habit of getting married. In the encounter with Jesus she lets herself be touched, changed and loved by him. Within a few hours she has become a missionary for him.

It is the story of someone who gets up one morning suspecting and expecting nothing. The day ends with her a totally changed person. She lets Jesus encounter, challenge and reveal himself to her.

(4) A student of mine once told me how he met a girl at a baseball game. After they chatted for a while, the topic of religion came up. "What are you?" he asked. She looked miserable and said: "A Catholic—worse luck."

Sometimes it can seem that believing in Christ forces us to lead half-lives. Accepting him—or at least accepting him *and* his commu-nity—appears to stop us from becoming fully human and condemn us to a deadly, unfree existence.

27

In John 4:46–53 *an officer in the royal service* leaves Capernaum and seeks Jesus out at Cana. He meets Jesus because he wants one particular thing—a cure for his sick son. The official gets not only what he wants but much more as well. He and his entire household become believers. Meeting Jesus leads him to found a community of faith.

What happens to that man goes far beyond his hopes and expectations. The official from Capernaum could never say "I believed in Jesus—worse luck."

Let us note some further precious details in the story of this encounter with the man from Capernaum. As we saw, earlier in John's Gospel Jesus speaks to Nicodemus of *rebirth to new life* and to the Samaritan woman of a *living water* which springs up to eternal life. In the cure of the official's son *life is restored.* This theme of life will continue in what Jesus will *say* later about the bread of life (6:25–59) and in what he will *do* in bringing Lazarus back to life (11:1–44). Jesus is in the business of giving us life and giving it in rich abundance.

A lovely detail which one could easily miss concerns the person whose son is cured. The Gospel gives him various names, calling him first an "official" (4:46. 49), then "the man" or rather "that human being" (4:50) and, finally, "the father" (4:53). He enters the story as what he is in public life—an official who carries out a state function. Then he becomes "the man" who believes the word which Jesus addresses to him. In meeting Jesus he loses, as it were, his public mask. He is simply a human being, face to face with the Lord. He is offered and accepts the only gift which matters: "The man believed the word that Jesus spoke to him."

Then he becomes "the father." His new faith has not reduced but reinforced his humanity. He is no longer merely an "official" but "the father" who goes back to his family and finds his son restored to health.

Then "all his household" also comes to believe. So far from being a private, isolating force, faith speaks out, spreads itself and builds communities of believers. What had been just a household now becomes a household of faith.

"Help us to face you and believe in you, Jesus. Help us to trust that by dropping our public masks and accepting you, we will find our lives enriched, our homes healed and our greatest blessings granted."

(5) The setting now switches to the pool of Bethesda in Jerusalem and *a man who has been ill for thirty-eight years* (5:1–18). He fell sick before Jesus was born. The man lies there—incurable and incredibly helpless. During the early years of his illness he could hope for healing, but now his friends have abandoned him and he has given up on himself. The sick man is the impotent slave of his own condition. He has become utterly used to the way he is.

He cannot move himself and go looking for Jesus, as Nicodemus and the official from Capernaum do. Jesus simply turns up and stands there looking at the sick man. In that great crowd of invalids (5:4) Jesus picks out the one who seems most in need. The others can to some extent help themselves, but this man has been ill so long that he cannot do anything for himself and has lost all heart.

What does the sick man expect when he notices Jesus gazing at him? Some food or some alms perhaps? Instead Jesus tries to rouse a little hope by asking, "Do you want to be healed?" The man reacts rather by making excuses for himself: "Sir, I have no man to put me into the pool when the water is troubled, and while I am going another steps down before me."

The sick man's situation has been tragically paradoxical. He has lived so close to a pool which every now and then possesses miraculous powers of healing. Yet he has been so ill and weak that he could not take the small step which would have saved him.

Jesus has singled out the sick man, tried to rouse some hope, made him acknowledge his impotence, and now he heals him: "Rise, take up your stretcher, and walk." With that the man who could not even move himself carries off his bed. He is healed and can resume a normal life.

But the story does not end there. The man is not yet fully healed. As the Gospel subtly puts it, he does not "know" Jesus (5:13). Unless he really knows Jesus, he will not be truly saved. Jesus seeks him out, in order to heal him interiorly: "See, you are well! Sin no more, that nothing worse befall you." Does the man recognize his own sinfulness, come to know Jesus in faith, and spread that faith? Rather he becomes the first betrayer, a kind of anticipation of Judas in the Fourth Gospel. For he goes to those who are outraged that this healing has occurred on the sabbath. He informs them that it is Jesus of Nazareth who was responsible for his cure. This strengthens their desire to kill Jesus (5:18).

Here is the first time John's Gospel clearly mentions any murderous plans to do away with Jesus. This chilling news comes in the aftermath of a living initiative from Jesus which has succeeded in touching the sick man's body but not his heart. Meeting Jesus and even being physically healed by him do not infallibly and irresistibly transform a human life.

(6) The next encounter with Jesus I want to discuss (7:53–8:11) has no fixed and secure place in the text of John. Some ancient authorities insert the story in the previous chapter or at the very end of the Gospel. Others omit the passage altogether or give it a home in Luke's Gospel. It is all rather like *the woman caught in adultery* herself.

Unlike the case of Nicodemus, the Samaritan woman and other individuals who encounter Jesus, we are told nothing about her background. Has she been locked into a long-standing affair? Was it a sudden act of passion? Was her husband out to catch her? Has she ever heard of Jesus? How will she relate to him later? About what has gone on before and what will follow afterward, we are given no details.

31

The woman meets Jesus because she is dragged or driven into his presence. What does she expect? That he will lead the stoning party? She says very little—just a brief "No one, Lord" when she is left alone with Jesus and he asks, "Woman, where are they? Has no one condemned you?" Jesus himself refuses to condemn or destroy her. He sends her away with one request, "Do not sin again." From the threat of death she has passed to the gift of new life.

The passage has a precarious place in the New Testament. But it records a very old story about an encounter with Jesus. That lifts it from oblivion, just as the woman's meeting with Jesus saves her too from oblivion.

In Rome and its surroundings I sometimes visit places Horace wrote about, and I remember his confident hope "Non omnis moriar" (I shall not wholly die). In a sense that old Horace never entertained, the thought bears applying to Jesus and ourselves. Like that woman caught in adultery—provided we find ourselves in Jesus' presence, even if we have to be dragged or driven there—we can hope that we will not wholly perish in oblivion but will be lifted from destruction.

(7) His disciples are with him when Jesus first meets *the man who has been blind from birth* (9:1–41). They see the poor man sitting there and begging, but show themselves quite blind to his misery and also to the power of Jesus. They do not ask their master to intervene. Rather they treat the blind man as a good occasion for a the-

ological discussion: "Rabbi, who sinned, this man or his parents, that he was born blind?"

The blind man does not say anything, let alone ask for a cure. Somehow he already knows Jesus' name (9:11) and presumably is heartened by what he hears Jesus say.

> It was not that this man sinned, or his parents, but that the works of God might be made manifest in him. We must work the works of him who sent me, while it is day; night comes, when no one can work. As long as I am in the world, *I am the light of the world.*

Then Jesus takes the initiative and anoints the blind man's eyes with clay. Now the blind man has something to do. He must go and wash his eyes in the pool of Siloam. He does that and comes back seeing for the first time in his life.

At this point Jesus has left the stage, so to speak. In the Fourth Gospel there is no other passage in which he is so long offstage (9:7b–34). But the man who now sees fills the scene as he begins to speak and act with simple vigor. He begins also to suffer in new ways.

Encountering Jesus means pain as well as healing. The man born blind would have learned to cope with his situation. Then Jesus comes along to heal him, but also to disturb his relationship with his parents and bring him into conflict with the religious authorities (9:13–34).

But the man born blind moves from truth to truth. He first recognizes "the man called Jesus" (9:11) as "a prophet" (9:17) and "from God" (9:33). Finally, he worships Jesus and expresses his faith: "Lord, I believe" (9:38). His encounter with Jesus has evolved steadily to that climax. What leads him there is his willingness *to trust his own experience.* The religious authorities badger him and in the name of God's sacred laws try to force him to agree that Jesus is a sinner. After all, the healing work has taken place on the sabbath. But the man born blind stands his ground and insists on what he has experienced: "Whether he is a sinner, I do not know; one thing I know, that though I was blind, now I see." Further reflection on this experience makes him realize the startling nature of what has happened: "Never since the world began has it been heard that anyone opened the eyes of a man born blind. If this man were not from God, he could do nothing." When Jesus returns to search for him, the man born blind is ready to confess his faith.

Chapter 9 of John's Gospel presents a scene of universal blindness. There is the man born blind himself. The disciples of Jesus do not see the truth (9:1f). Some Pharisees are likewise spiritually blind (9:39–41). At the level of language the chapter is dominated by words for blindness, eyes and sight. Among all those terms one recurrent phrase, "to open the eyes" (9:10. 14. 17. 21. 26. 30. 32), points ahead most clearly to the great conclusion. We can believe ourselves to see and presume ourselves to have spiritual insight. But it

34

is only when we acknowledge that we are spiritually blind and ask for help that our eyes will be opened by Jesus who is the light of the world.

(8) *The raising of Lazarus* (11:1–44) portrays an encounter at the limit. To be sure, Jesus also meets Martha and Mary. But the great encounter is with his friend Lazarus who is dead and decomposing in the grave.

Obviously Lazarus can have no expectations that Jesus will do something for him. Nor do his two sisters expect anything. Jesus has come too late. Martha goes straight to the point: "Lord, if you had been here, my brother would not have died." She then takes back somewhat the sting of that reproach by adding, "Even now I know that whatever you ask from God, God will give you." Nevertheless, when Jesus visits the tomb and asks for the stone to be taken away from the entrance, Martha protests: "Lord, by this time there will be an odor, for he has been dead four days." Humanly speaking, the situation is ultimately and absolutely hopeless.

But with his loud cry "Lazarus, come out," Jesus intervenes to transform a family tragedy. We have seen him heal situations of *slavery* (the invalid in Chapter 5) and of *darkness* (the blind man in Chapter 9). Now he heals a situation of *death*. He reveals himself as "the resurrection and the life." Lazarus has "fallen asleep" (11:11), but there is no way he will wake up unless Jesus steps in to bring him back from the sleep of death.

Various emotions color the whole episode. The disciples of Jesus express their fear over the

35

dangers involved in going to Bethany (11:8. 16). Mary weeps at Jesus' feet. When he sees that, he also breaks down and cries. But the dominant feeling and force is neither fear nor grief, but love and the disclosure of love in action.

The chapter begins by insisting on the "horizontal" love which binds Jesus to Martha, Mary and their brother Lazarus (11:3. 5. 11), and suggests also Jesus' bond of "vertical" love with the Father (11:41f). That powerful love now sets Lazarus free from death and gives him new life. When he comes forth from the tomb, others have to "unbind him, and let him go." But Jesus' love has already unbound Lazarus and loved him into life.

Besides setting free and giving life, love also brings together what is separated. Sickness and death have broken up the family at Bethany. Jesus' love now reunites Lazarus with his sisters.

Such love is a high risk. Here its results provoke Caiaphas and the other Jerusalem authorities into taking their decision of "expediency"— Jesus must die (11:50). His love costs him his life. At the end of the Gospel Peter protests his love ("Lord, you know everything; you know that I love you"), only to be warned at once that the price of such real love is death (21:17–19).

Paul Goodman once said that the only way for a Christian to live is to risk love and hope for resurrection. As an Australian writer, Peter Steele, commented, "He assumed, rightly, that love will pin us to the cross and that crucifixion has only one outcome."

In his *Spiritual Exercises* (n. 285) St. Ignatius Loyola adds a significant phrase to the cry of Jesus in John 11:43: "Come out, Lazarus, *to my side.*" Of course, these words are not as such those of John. But where else could one go who has been raised by Jesus from death? In any case the Ignatian addition is not so foreign to the Gospel, which notes what Lazarus goes on to do and to endure. Not only does he join his sisters in hosting Jesus at a special, pre-Passover supper (12:1ff), but also he shares in the threat which is looming over Jesus' head: "The chief priests planned to put Lazarus also to death, because on account of him many of the Jews were going away and believing in Jesus" (12:10f). Lazarus has been raised from the dead, only to stand beside his friend Jesus as the passion bears down on them.

In the whole encounter with Jesus, Lazarus acts, is threatened, and never speaks. Like the others who meet Jesus he encourages us to place ourselves spiritually in the story. Am I a dead Lazarus, bound and quietly corrupting in a sealed tomb—someone over whom people can only shake their heads and say, "Poor O'Collins, there's no helping him now"? Or am I a Lazarus already shuffling my way toward the door and the light? Or have I been fully awakened, raised and freed, so that I can genuinely stand at Jesus' side?

At this stage it will do no harm to pause, take stock, and pray. The encounters with Andrew, the Samaritan woman and the royal official highlight the path to *faith*. In Chapter 9 a blind man comes to the *light*. In Chapter 11 Jesus' *love* proves more powerful than the death which has overcome his friend.

Jesus,
by the light of the faith
which you have given us,
may we accept your powerful love,
and come to stand with you,
our dearest friend.

(9) In John's Gospel the pattern of meetings with individuals goes on after the crucifixion and resurrection. The risen Jesus keeps up the old habit. Let me take two examples: *the disciple whom Jesus loves* and *Mary Magdalene*.

(a) Even nowadays—or should I say especially nowadays?—the sight of two people very much in love still delights us. The world continues to love and make excuses for lovers. A truly great love story will fill the cinemas and top the list of best-sellers. Yet the modern world has come to believe that love is blind. In their delirious joy lovers are supposed to be incapable of seeing how things really are.

Not everyone, however, has accepted our modern prejudice. "Give me a lover," St. Augustine exclaimed, "and he will understand." Augustine realized that it may take deep love to open our eyes and let us see the truth. The heart does have its reasons. Love helps us to know and share in reality. We meet and know Jesus through love.

In two episodes (20:2–10; 21:1–14) the beloved disciple is mysteriously led by love to encounter Jesus truly risen from the dead. He enters the empty tomb, sees the grave cloths and believes (20:8). Love makes the beloved disciple jump at once to the right conclusion: Jesus has risen and is alive.

In the second scene the beloved disciple is one of seven disciples who have spent a night out fishing in Lake Tiberias. At dawn they all look across the waters toward the stranger who calls to them from the beach. But love allows the beloved disciple to identify who it is that has come to meet them at daybreak: "It is the Lord" (21:7). Once again love brings him to know the truth and recognize the risen Jesus.

The beloved disciple *sees* an empty tomb and reaches out in faith to the risen Lord. He *hears* a voice at dawn across the waters of a lake and knows himself to be in Jesus' presence. Our lives are full of sights and sounds. Love can turn those sights and sounds into moments when we cry out: "It is the Lord."

"Jesus, give us a heart to love you with. Then we shall truly see you, encounter you constantly, and recklessly believe in you."

(b) Mary Magdalene meets the living Jesus because she has come back to the tomb looking for his dead body. The tears flood down her face (20:11. 13. 15). She now finds two angels sitting in the tomb like a guard of honor. She does not ask them for any help or information, but simply explains why she is weeping and turns her back on them. In her grief and love she is anxious only to locate the corpse of Jesus which "they" have taken away and laid somewhere.

Then Mary sees the "gardener" standing there in the garden outside the new tomb where he had been buried (see 19:41). It is the risen Jesus, the new Adam who is inaugurating his new creation. Artists like Fra Angelico or Rembrandt have sensed something about that encounter which theologians have missed: its joyful playfulness. They depict Jesus as wearing a gardener's hat or with a tool slung over his shoulder. His disguise delays briefly the moment of recognition.

Mary imagines that the "gardener" might have carried off the body, but expects that all the same he would be ready to help her: "Sir, if you have carried him away, tell me where you have laid him, and I will take him away." Then with one word Jesus changes her life. He calls her by name, "Mary."

John's Gospel has made much of Mary's grief over the disappearance of Jesus' corpse. She has been weeping outside the tomb; she has been weeping as she stooped to look into the tomb. The two angels and then the risen Jesus himself have asked the reason for her tears. Now she knows him to be gloriously alive. But apart from telling us that she clings to Jesus, the Gospel makes no attempt to capture her joy in a net of words. It is the same with the raising of Lazarus. John notes the tears and grief of Martha, Mary and Jesus himself over the death of Lazarus, but discreetly declines to portray their happiness over his return to life.

In the Fourth Gospel no other encounter with Jesus matches the contrast between Mary Magdalene's expectations and the outcome. She expects at most to be helped to find a missing corpse. Instead she learns that death has no final power over Jesus, and that she is to bring to the disciples the ultimate good news: "I have seen the Lord."

This chapter has pulled in examples of encounters between Jesus and representative individuals. Some meet him because they have gone looking for him (Nicodemus, the royal official). One person seemingly by chance blunders into his presence (the Samaritan woman). Another is dragged or driven to see him (the woman caught in adultery). Others again encounter him because he himself comes to them (the man sick for thirty-eight years, the man blind from birth, Lazarus). Andrew and his companion are directed toward Jesus.

All in all, it does not seem to matter very much *how* these and others in John's Gospel happen to meet Jesus. The only important thing is that first they *do* find themselves in his presence and that then they *respond* to his initiatives. Except for the invalid in 5:1–18, all the individuals we have looked at allow Jesus to take over. Andrew and his companion let Jesus lead them away for a quiet afternoon together. Nicodemus

41

lets Jesus take up some surprisingly new themes. The Samaritan woman lets Jesus not only raise the touchy topic of her irregular life but also gradually reveal himself to her. Lastly, Mary Magdalene lets him call her by name.

In every case what Jesus does goes far beyond the expectations of those who encounter him. Some, like the Samaritan woman, the man born blind or, for that matter, the dead Lazarus, have no hopes or expectations whatsoever when they meet Jesus. Nicodemus wants a little theological reassurance. The royal official is looking only for a specific miracle of healing. Mary Magdalene merely expects a little help in locating a stolen corpse. Whatever the given expectations, Jesus always does something more, calls for something different, and dramatically changes the lives of those who meet him.

Instinctively we probably suppose that it is a good thing to have great expectations—to borrow a title from Charles Dickens. Realistically we will also probably admit that we may be inclined to have low expectations or few expectations—especially about ourselves. "O'Collins, yesterday, today and the same forever. G. O'C, as he was in the beginning, is now and ever shall be, faults and sins without end."

If I am right about this, we can, nevertheless, take comfort from the encounters with Jesus in John's Gospel. They suggest that prior expectations will not prove decisive, *provided* we somehow get into Jesus' presence. We may be dragged into his presence, walk there, blunder into meeting him, or simply find that he is standing before us. If then we let him take over, the rest will follow.

We may like Nicodemus respond slowly to his initiatives. Or we may open ourselves up quickly like the Samaritan woman. Either way, as long as we open the door and even cautiously let Jesus in, he will change our lives and his promise is a certainty: "Whoever drinks of the water that I shall give him will never thirst; the water that I shall give him will become in him a spring of water welling up to eternal life."

# JESUS IN SPACE AND TIME

# 3

# *Jesus in Space and Prayer*

The Gospel of John is a school of prayer. One can rightly interpret it as a great act of contemplation that sweeps from the community's response at the beginning to an individual's adoration at the end: from "the Word became flesh and we have contemplated his glory" (1:14) to Thomas' confession, "My Lord and my God" (20:28).

I propose to reflect on two themes (Jesus as center of our spiritual space and the various Johannine images of him), and then take up very directly the matter of prayer.

## I

(1) Right from the first chapter and the question of the two disciples (*"Where* are you stay-

ing?''), John represents faith as a *movement* toward Jesus as the center of our spiritual space. For the two disciples, seeing *where* Jesus lives becomes a remaining *with* him (1:39).

At the climax of the Gospel Mary Magdalene searches for the missing body of her master. She does not know *"where* they/you have laid him" (20:2. 13. 15). Perhaps no other chapter brings out so exquisitely the various dimensions of the movement believers make—or are led to make—toward Jesus. The beloved disciple and Peter, Mary Magdalene herself, the disciples in the upper room, and Thomas express different components of that movement.

At some point faith entails a movement from *ignorance* to a *recognition* of the divine designs recorded and revealed by the Bible. Initially Peter and the beloved disciple do "not yet know the scripture, that he must rise from the dead" (20:9).

Then for Mary Magdalene faith means a movement from *absence* to *presence*. She shifts from terrible desolation over the loss of Jesus to radiant joy at Jesus refound.

The disciples hide in fear behind shut doors. Their resurrection faith involves a passage from anxious *fear* in the face of a threatening world to *peace* and *joy* in the Lord's presence. "Jesus . . . said to them, 'Peace be with you.' . . . Then the disciples were glad when they saw the Lord." He has come to stand among them, show them himself, breathe the life of new creation into them, and empower them with the Holy Spirit for their coming mission.

48

Lastly, faith brings that movement from lonely *doubt* to adoring *certainty.* The transformation of Thomas is the paradigm example.

In sum, faith and the prayer of faith involve constantly re-enacting the spiritual "passage" of John 20. We are ever moving toward Jesus to find peace, joy and certainty in his presence, as well as an insight into the Scriptures that illuminates the flux of little crucifixions and resurrections which make up the tissue of our lives.

(2) The Jesus of the Fourth Gospel is presented in three characteristic ways: as *the cosmic Principle, the divine Lord,* and *the intimate Friend.* The images are not clearly distinguished from each other, and they do not cover all the ways that Jesus is portrayed in this Gospel, but they do suggest typical plctures of him that we experience in prayer and life.

First, Jesus Christ is the Logos, the all-pervading and ultimate Principle of creation, meaning and order. He is the deepest ground of things, the creative Word, the wisdom which permeates the universe. Here is the light of the world, that light which shines mysteriously in the hearts of all men and women who come into existence. This is the Word through whom, in whom and for whom all things were created. "He is before all things, and in him all things hold together" (Col 1:16f).

This first image depicts Christ as the cosmic Power and Presence, the Omega-point toward which everything and everyone will converge.

A brief saying I read once on a Christmas

card catches the second Johannine image: "Jesus is Lord, Jesus is King, Jesus is our everything." Here he is seen in a more definable, albeit divine, way. This is the Jesus of Nathanael's confession in Chapter 1 ("You are the Son of God! You are the King of Israel") and of Thomas' confession in Chapter 20 ("My Lord and my God").

Lastly, Jesus is the intimate friend of the family at Bethany. He is the one who lets Mary anoint his feet with ointment and wipe them with her hair (11:2; 12:3). The disciple whom he loves reclines close to him at the Last Supper (13:23. 25). After the resurrection Jesus wants to hear Peter three times affirm his loving friendship. Only then as friend to friend does he trustingly invite Peter, "Follow me" (21:19. 22).

These three images of Jesus mutually complement and correct each other. In isolation they could be misused. By itself the first might end up representing Christ as mere impersonal force. The second could lapse into making him a distant, authoritarian figure. The third can fall apart through self-indulgent sentimentality. Taken together, however, the three images interpret one another and present a Jesus who is at once the Logos, Lord and Lover of us all.


II


(1) Very often the language of prayer is simple and repetitive. The "Jesus Prayer" of Eastern

Christianity and the Old Testament psalms illustrate that truth; there are many other similar traditions both Christian and non-Christian.

The Fourth Gospel has a vocabulary of just over one thousand words—as compared with Paul who uses well over two thousand words in his letters. John has built much of his Gospel out of simple words—often one-syllable or two-syllable (Greek) terms—which recur over and over again: "light," "life," "glory," "Father," "truth," "I am," and so forth. "Light" turns up twenty-three times, "life" thirty-six times, and "glory" eighteen times. "Father" is applied to God one hundred and eighteen times. (In Matthew's Gospel this happens forty-five times.)

The simple, repetitive vocabulary of John forms and fashions a mood of prayer. It holds the reader's attention on certain luminous truths which form the central themes of the Gospel.

This vocabulary facilitates *the stark contrasts* we find in John: light/darkness, truth/lie, belief/rejection, love/hatred, life/death, the glory of God/the glory of men. This Gospel demands *a total response* from the prayerful reader. One must wholeheartedly choose light over darkness, life over death and so on.

In his simple but utterly profound way John has said everything he wants to say when he writes, "The Word became flesh and dwelt among us." The opening verses really contain all that will follow in the Gospel: "In him was life, and the life was the light of men." To be sure, we need to be taken through the ministry, passion, crucifixion and resurrection of Jesus, so that we can make progress in assimilating it all. But once we truly *know* what those simple words mean at the beginning of the Gospel—"we have contemplated his glory, the glory of the Father's only Son"—we already know the whole mystery. *The point of departure will then be the point of arrival.*

Here it is worth noting a certain parallel between John and Ignatius Loyola's *Spiritual Exercises*. Their simple, repetitive vocabulary constantly presents us with stark contrasts. Right from the outset Ignatius asks for a total response from the retreatant. The very first "Annotation" or introductory observation indicates the overall aim. It is not just to reduce one's "inordinate attachments" or free oneself completely from some of them. Ignatius expects that the Exercises will "prepare and dispose the soul *to rid itself* of *all* inordinate attachments" (italics mine). Lastly, the "First Principle and Foundation" which comes at the start of the Exercises like the prologue to John's Gospel really contains everything that will follow. Those who follow the Exercises right through to the "Contemplation for Obtaining Love" do not ultimately know "more" than is expressed and implied by the simple, luminous logic of Ignatius' prologue, the "First Principle and Foundation."

(2) As a good school of Christian prayer, John's Gospel provides us with examples of various kinds of *prayers made to Jesus himself*. There

are requests for oneself or for others: "They have no wine" (2:3); "Give me this water, that I may not thirst" (4:15); "Lord, show us the Father, and we shall be satisfied" (14:8). There are complaints and cries of pain: "Lord, if you had been here, my brother would not have died" (11:32). There are professions of faith from the utterly simple "Lord, I believe" of the man born blind (9:38) to Peter's "Lord, to whom shall we go? You have the words of eternal life; and we have believed, and have come to know, that you are the Holy One of God" (6:68f). There are prayers of hope: "I know that he will rise again in the resurrection at the last day" (11:24). Finally, there are protestations of love: "Lord, you know everything; you know that I love you" (21:17).

The "I am" sayings, which are such a feature of the Fourth Gospel, closely align themselves with the prayers explicitly made to Jesus. Such sayings occur over fifty times: "I am the bread of life"; "I am the light of the world"; "I am the resurrection and the life"; "I am the way, the truth and the life"; and so forth. These "I am" sayings slip ever so easily into formulas for praising and thanking Jesus for what he is.

> You are the bread of life;
> you are the light of the world;
> you are our resurrection and our life.
> You are the way to walk,
> the truth to practice
> and the life to be filled with.

(3) John also sets out Jesus' own prayers to the Father. Before raising Lazarus, Jesus lifts his eyes and says: "Father, I thank you that you have heard me. I know that you always hear me, but I have said this on account of the people standing by, that they may believe that you sent me" (11:41f). Before his passion Jesus prays in distress. This is the only time that John's Gospel records an audible response from heaven:

> "Now is my soul troubled. And what shall I say? 'Father, save me from this hour'? No, for this purpose I have come to this hour. Father, glorify your name." Then a voice came from heaven, "I have glorified it, and I will glorify it again" (12:27f).

That response becomes the opening part of Jesus' great prayer before his arrest: "Father, the hour has come; glorify your Son that the Son may glorify you" (17:1). This prayer to the Father, which takes up the whole of Chapter 17, is far and away the longest prayer by Jesus found in any of the Gospels. Significantly the prayer ends with a plea that we may be drawn into the mysterious life of the divine love—"that the love with which you have loved me may be in them, and I in them."

(4) To complete this sketch of prayer in the Fourth Gospel, we should also note *Jesus' direct teaching on prayer*. In his last discourse he indi-

cates both how we should pray and what we can expect from our prayer.

We pray, first of all, "in the name of" Jesus (14:13f). This means turning to the Father and identifying ourselves with the One from whom our salvation comes (15:16; 16:23f). The liturgy captures this point perfectly by constantly praying "through Christ our Lord."

When we identify ourselves with Jesus and his teaching, we can be confident that our prayer will be heard: "If you abide in me, and my words abide in you, ask whatever you will, and it shall be done for you" (15:7). This goes decisively beyond what we are told in the other Gospels: "Ask, and it will be given you; seek, and you will find; knock and it will be opened to you" (Mt 7:7; see Mk 11:24). In the Fourth Gospel, Jesus calls on us to identify with him, share his filial trust and abandon ourselves in him to his Father. Then "if you ask anything of the Father, he will give it to you in my name" (16:23).

At the beginning of the Gospels two of the disciples decided to "remain *with*" Jesus (1:39). In the Eucharistic discourse all disciples are invited to receive the bread of life and "remain *in*" Jesus: "He who eats my flesh and drinks my blood abides in me, and I in him" (6:56). Then in the final discourse Jesus calls on them to live *in* him and *to pray from that vantage-point.*

This kind of praying not merely with but also in and through Jesus anticipates our final state— "that day" when our identification with him will be completed: "In that day you will know that I am in the Father, and you in me, and I in you" (14:20).

To pray, therefore, is to identify ourselves trustingly with Jesus himself, and to know that what we are doing is mysteriously bringing about now what will be fully unfolded at the end.

# CRUCIFIXION AND RESURRECTION

# 4

# Crucifixion and Resurrection

On his way to martyrdom in Rome St. Ignatius of Antioch called the crucifixion a mystery which took place "in the silence of God" (Letter to the Ephesians, 19). Apropos of Good Friday and Easter Sunday, long, wordy commentaries achieve little. In fact they may only distract us from the mystery of Jesus' dying and rising. What springs from a silent, reverent reading of the Gospel texts promises to do more toward touching our hearts.

Such quiet, prayerful pondering of the passion story is part of being *with* Jesus *where he is for me:* "If anyone serves me, he must follow me; and where I am, there shall my servant be also" (12:26).

So I do not wish here to offer some massively detailed treatment of the last chapters in John's Gospel. Rather I prefer to pick out some moments in the whole story and let the paschal mystery speak through them.

I

(1) Some pious Greeks tell the disciple Philip: "Sir, we wish to *see* Jesus" (12:22). When Jesus hears about this request, he does not answer it directly but speaks of his passion. They will be able *to see him* all right—lifted high on his cross. That will be the place where we can all see him. "They shall look on him whom they have pierced" (19:37). It takes seven chapters for those Greeks to have their reply. When it comes, it comes at Golgotha.

(2) "Truly, truly, *I say to you,* unless a grain of wheat falls into the earth and dies, it remains alone; but if it dies, it bears much fruit" (12:24). But Jesus says it also to himself. He submits to this general "law." Why should the Son of God have to submit to such a law? Perhaps it is thoroughly acceptable as a biological law or even as some law for human beings: living results come through loss, suffering self-abandonment and even death. But why has the Son of God to verify personally the "principle" that the crucifixion is "the price of progress"?

(3) "Walk while you have the light, lest the darkness overtake you" (12:35). Jesus himself does just that, getting to Calvary on time before darkness falls over the whole earth (Mk 15:33).

(4) "Now before the feast of the Passover . . . Jesus knew that his hour had come to depart out of this world to the Father" (13:1). Time was running out fast. Even so Jesus first washed his disciples' feet (13:2–11), gave them his last, intimate instructions (13:12–16:33), and only then turned in trusting prayer to his Father (17:1–26).

Others have washed and anointed Jesus' feet (11:2; 12:3; Lk 7:36f; etc.). Now, right at the end, Jesus performs this task for his friends. What are we to make of this? Is the Son of God at our service?

"Jesus, knowing that the Father had given all things into his *hands* . . . got up from supper" (13:3f). Within and through the life of the Trinity, all things were in his hands, and yet he took into those hands our feet—to wash them. After that he stretched out those same hands to be nailed to a cross.

"But afterward you will understand (13:7). We have been trying to understand it all ever since—that Jesus wants to serve us, that he loves us and gave himself up for us.

A sense of Judas' presence runs through the whole episode of the washing of the disciples' feet (13:2. 10f. 18). Of all those individuals in John's Gospel who play a role in Jesus' death (Caiaphas, Annas and Pilate), Judas is the one we know best *and least.* He is the shadow side of us all. If he had not existed, it would have been necessary to invent him.

"Do you know what I have done to you?"

(13:12). Jesus asks *that* question. He might very well ask: "Do you know what you/they are about to do *to me?*"

John's Gospel contains only two beatitudes. One concerns faith: "Blessed are those who have not seen and yet believe" (20:29). The other beatitude is refreshingly candid about practice.

> If I then, your Lord and Teacher, have washed your feet, you also ought to wash one another's feet. For I have given you an example, that you also should do as I have done to you. . . . A servant is no greater than his master; nor is he who is sent greater than he who sent him. If you know these things, *blessed are you if you do them* (13:14–17).

(5) The only commandment recorded by John is the "new commandment" of love among the disciples (13:34; 15:12. 17). The Fourth Gospel has the earlier discourse on the bread of life (6:25–59), but at the end it does not include the institution of the Eucharist. Instead it names mutual love as the deepest meaning of the Eucharist.

Some liturgies of Eastern Christianity make the same point. At the central moment of the Eucharist they proclaim the new commandment of love.

(6) Jesus urges his friends, "Let not *your* hearts be troubled" (14:1), when his own heart is deeply troubled (13:21). He comforts them with the promise, "I go to prepare a place for you." Then "I will come again and take you to myself,

that where I am you may be also" (14:2f). His death by crucifixion becomes simply a matter of "going to prepare a place" for us. It is almost unbearably painful to hear him describe Calvary that way.

In the last discourse Jesus is full of realism *and* tender compassion. He bluntly warns Peter of his coming breakdown (13:38). But at once he adds: "Let not your hearts be troubled" (14:1). Jesus stands up like a great tree—realistic and compassionate, even though he is already under the shadow of the cross.

(7) "I am the way, and the truth, and the life" (14:6).

> Without you, Jesus, there is no real traveling.
> We go nowhere.
> Without you, Jesus, there is no truth.
> All is falsehood.
> Without you, Jesus, there is no living.
> There is only death.
> We adore you, O Christ, and we praise you,
> because by your holy way
> you have redeemed the world.
> We adore you, O Christ, and we praise you,
> because by your holy truth
> you have enlightened the world.
> We adore you, O Christ, and we praise you,
> because by your holy life
> you have shared with us everlasting life.

(8) Jesus sees the crucifixion as being glorified, as glorifying the Father (17:2), as accomplishing the work given him by the Father (17:4),

and as bringing God's sons and daughters into unity (17:22f). Out of the ugly horror of Calvary Jesus expects to bring the glorious and crowning success of human unity in God.

(9) Judas leads the soldiers to the garden where "Jesus often met with his disciples" (18:2). They came to make the arrest in a place that was special and holy for Jesus and his friends.

(10) Pilate asks Jesus: "*What* have you done?" (18:35). Jesus does not answer the question directly. When he comes to the point of death, he will exclaim, "*It* is finished" (19:30). The "what" and "it" remain unspecified. Each one of us has to acknowledge for himself or herself just what it is Jesus has done and finished.

(11) The encounter between Jesus and Pilate forms a great central section of the passion story (18:28—19:16). It is carefully constructed around seven scenes which have a chiastic structure.

$a^1$ Pilate comes out to meet the accusers (18:29–32).
$b^1$ —— Pilate goes back to speak with Jesus (18:33–38a).
$c^1$ ———— Pilate comes out again to the accusers (18:38b–40).
d ————— Jesus is scourged and crowned (19:1–3).
$c^2$ ———— Pilate comes out to present Jesus (19:4–8).
$b^2$ —— Pilate goes back to speak again with Jesus (19:9–12a).
$a^2$ Pilate comes out to condemn Jesus (19:12b–16).

Admittedly, we can read off the meaning of this elaborate pattern in different ways. We might see it all as building up to a climax in a$^2$, the scene when Pilate finally presents Jesus: "Behold your King!" Although the chief priests reject Jesus ("We have no king but Caesar") and secure his execution, the believing reader knows that in and through the passion Jesus truly reigns as our King. He rules from the tree of the cross.

Another clear possibility is to identify scene d as the heart of the matter. There Jesus suffers the awful pain and humiliation of the scourging and the crowning with thorns.

> Then Pilate took Jesus and scourged him. And the soldiers plaited a crown of thorns, and put it on his head, and arrayed him in a purple robe; they came up to him, saying, "Hail, King of the Jews!" and struck him with their hands.

Whatever way we interpret the pattern, we will certainly catch more of John's nuances if we see scene d as standing a little by itself and read together the other matching scenes: a$^1$ with a$^2$, b$^1$ with b$^2$, and c$^1$ with c$^2$.

(12) When Jesus is crucified, Pilate and the chief priests argue about the title on the cross (19:19–22), and the soldiers work out how Jesus' clothing will be shared (19:23f), but Jesus himself speaks only to his mother and the beloved disciple (19:25–27).

(13) John has told us that Jesus should die "to

gather into one the children of God who are scattered" (11:52). When it does happen, we see the children of God beginning to gather there around the cross. Jesus' mother, two other women and the beloved disciple have witnessed his crucifixion and death. Now Joseph of Arimathea and Nicodemus arrive to take down the body and give Jesus a royal burial. This tiny group of three women and three men will grow to be an enormous multitude who gather together to kiss the wounds of the Son of Man and pray: "We adore you, O Christ, and we praise you, because by your holy cross you have redeemed the world."

II

In previous chapters I have already drawn on the two final chapters of John. It would be tedious to repeat what has been said. Let me rather sketch impressionistically what John yields for the second half of the paschal mystery.

(1) One small but significant detail emerges from the terminology. Jesus is risen from the dead, but in the two Easter chapters John never speaks explicitly of "appearances" and only twice refers as such to the resurrection (20:9; 21:14). Mary Magdalene, for example, is not asked to tell Jesus' brethren, "I am risen from the dead and will appear to you in Jerusalem. There you will see me." Rather the message she must carry to them is, "I am ascending to my Father and your Father, to my God and your God" (20:17). The

skeptical Thomas sums up his incredulity without referring to the resurrection as such: "Unless I see in his hands the print of the nails, and place my finger in the mark of the nails, and place my hand in his side, I will not believe" (20:25). Thomas does not explicitly say, "I will not believe that he is risen, unless he appears to me."

John's Easter language takes this form. Jesus is simply "standing" there when Mary Magdalene turns around (20:14). The disciples are gathered behind closed doors, when he simply "comes and stands among them" (20:19. 24. 26). By the Sea of Tiberias Jesus "reveals himself," "standing on the beach" at daybreak (21:1. 4. 15). Every time he comes, he speaks—to Mary Magdalene, to Thomas and the rest. The disciples respond to the Lord's presence by "seeing" him (20:18. 22. 29), by "knowing" that it is the Lord (21:12), by "believing" (20:29), by speaking with him, by announcing to others their experience of him, by receiving his gifts, by protesting their love, by following him and so forth.

Beyond question, John recognizes a real difference between (a) the experience of those first witnesses to whom the risen Lord appeared and (b) the experience of all later Christians (20:29). Nevertheless, not wishing to push this difference too far, he plays down the language of resurrection and appearances. Instead he uses simple terms that encourage us later Christians to identify, as far as possible, with what Mary Magdalene and the other disciples experience. The Lord will be "standing" there before us in every situation, even though we may fail at first to recognize him. He will "come and stand among us" when we hide fearfully behind closed doors. He wishes us to know his presence, believe, and follow him in the power of the Holy Spirit he breathes on us.

(2) John 20:1–18 serves as well as any other Gospel passage to illustrate how people with diverse mentalities and temperaments can all seek the Lord and the signs of his presence. Mary Magdalene is deeply affectionate; the beloved disciple is quick and intuitive; Peter is solid and slow. Their gifts are different, but they come together in their common quest for Jesus.

(3) When he meets Mary Magdalene, the risen Lord begins from *her* situation: "Woman, why are you weeping? Whom do you seek?" His exquisite client-centered counseling gradually rouses her faith. He takes the same approach with the two disciples on the road to Emmaus (Lk 24:13–35). They eventually "know" him "in the breaking of the bread." Mary knows him when he calls her by name.

Mary clings to him. Jesus tells her that he is changing his way of being present in the world. He is about to inaugurate the new order of the Holy Spirit. She must become used to his risen presence through the Spirit, which will reveal him in all the new situations of life in the emerging Church.

(4) Thomas is not going to see Jesus, unless and until he humbly spends time with the other disciples (20:26). Where was he the first time Jesus appeared to the disciples (20:24)? Out

bravely showing his face in Jerusalem or even in the temple? But to find Jesus courage is not enough.

(5) The appearance of Jesus at dawn (21:4) seems a reward for constancy. The seven disciples (including Thomas) have persevered at their common task through the night. At the end of their hard and "unsuccessful" work they find Jesus standing on the shore. Has he already been there right through the hours of darkness?

(6) Peter is to glorify God by a martyr's death (21:19). John who is related to Jesus by a special bond of love will "remain" until his master comes (21:20f). God is free not only to give more to some (John) but even to make greater demands on those who have received less (Peter).

# THE BLOOD OF THE LAMB

# 5

# *The Blood of the Lamb*

It has frequently been remarked that the passion narratives of John and the other Gospels are most sparing in their description of Jesus' physical sufferings. There is, for instance, only one reference to his shedding blood: this is to Jesus hanging on the cross with his side pierced by the soldier's lance—"and immediately there flowed out blood and water" (Jn 19:34).[1]

Unlike many other forms of dying, crucifixion involved a massive loss of blood. Years before John's Gospel took its final shape, other New Testament authors saw and recorded a redemptive significance in the bloody nature of Jesus' execution. The earliest Gospel recalled the Last Supper when Jesus took the cup and said, "This is my blood of the covenant, which is poured out for many" (Mk 14:24). A key Pauline passage spoke of Jesus "expiating" our sins through his blood

(Rom 3:25), and another passage saw that blood as "justifying" us (Rom 5:9). Through Christ God "chose to reconcile all things to himself, whether on earth or in heaven, making peace by the blood of his cross" (Col 1:20). First Peter assured its readers that they had been "ransomed" by "the precious blood of Christ" (1:18ff). The Letter to the Hebrews expounded the priestly service of Christ whose blood has purified us "to serve the living God" (9:12. 14; 13:12). The Book of Revelation pushed language to its limits when it "explained" that the heavenly multitude in white garments had "washed their robes and made them white in the blood of the Lamb" (7:14).

In some recent *translations* of the New Testament and theological writings, for whatever reason (squeamishness?), there seems to be an unwillingness to mention the blood of Jesus. No translation can expunge "blood" from John 19:34 where the whole point of the passage is that blood and water gushed out. Elsewhere, however, it is a different question. *Good News for Modern Man,* the New Testament in *Today's English Version,* repeatedly refuses to translate exactly references to Jesus' blood and often introduces a vaguer term, death. That version renders Colossians 1:20 as follows:

> Through the Son, then, God decided to bring the whole universe back to himself. God made peace through his Son's death on the cross, and so brought back to himself all both on earth and in heaven.

The *New English Bible* modifies Paul's concreteness in Romans 3:25 and calls Jesus "the means of expiating sin by his sacrificial death."

When contemporary *theological* works deal with the suffering and death of Jesus, they regularly fail to discuss how he made peace "through the shedding of his blood upon the cross" (Col 1:20). An easy way of verifying this sweeping judgment is to review the chapter (or sections) devoted to Jesus' death in recent Christologies coming from Europe, North America, Latin America and other parts of the world.

Among current writers Jürgen Moltmann, albeit that he belongs to a reformed Protestant tradition, risked being in a minority of one when he wrote of the Church being born from "the wounded side of Christ on Calvary." He quoted approvingly from Pope Pius XII's 1943 encyclical, *Mystici Corporis:* "Having established the Church in his blood, he [Christ] fortified it on the day of Pentecost with special power from on high."[2] But then apart from two passing references to the forgiveness of sins through the blood of Christ,[3] Moltmann had no more to say either of the piercing of Christ's corpse on the cross or of the blood and water which flowed from that wound. After a brief appearance John 19:34 was forgotten.

The current theological and exegetical "distaste" for the blood of Christ, at least among Catholics, is understandable if not fully excusable. One is reminded, for example, of the annual disquiet over the liquefaction of the blood of St. Januarius in Naples. M.-D. Chenu was one of the distinguished theological architects of the Second Vatican Council. Yet his article "Sang du Christ" in Volume 14 of the *Dictionnaire de Theologie Catholique* (Paris, 1939) indicates where "theological haematology" was stuck up to the recent past. Chenu describes how the generality of theologians agree that Christ's blood was personally united to the Word of God. He then lists the questions which remain open: Was the precious blood separated from the Word during the passion? If so, did it merit adoration? If Christ's blood has in fact been preserved as a relic, should we adore such a relic? Devotion to the blood of Christ had somehow become separated from the reality of his humanity and his historical life and death. We had devotion to the "five wounds," the Sacred Head as well as the Sacred Heart, as though these were separate objects of a quaint and primitive piety rather than integral to the entire mystery of Christ's redemption.

Yet, in spite of these exaggerations and the reactions to which they have given rise (for example, the feast of the Precious Blood, raised to a double of the first class in 1934, was suppressed altogether in 1969[4]), it is important for us to appreciate what it originally meant and still must mean today when it is proclaimed that Jesus effected "our peace and reconciliation" with God through shedding his blood in the crucifixion (Col 1:20). What I wish to do in this chapter is to reflect on what was symbolically expressed by the blood (and water) which flowed from the wounded side of Christ (Jn 19:34).

# THE JEWISH BACKGROUND

It is hardly possible, however, to grasp the symbolism of blood in early Christian thought and its Old Testament background without some workable typology. Otherwise the information is so complex and culturally conditioned that it threatens to frustrate any attempt at clear understanding and interpretation. So much diverse material is at hand to provide answers to the basic question: How did the Israelites think about blood in their relationship with God? It is true that pure or ideal types do not exist in our world; they belong, as the philosophers say, to an exaggerated realism. Nonetheless, typology can be useful, inasmuch as it helps both to classify the data on the religious symbolism of blood and to elaborate some kind of ordered understanding. For example, it is simple enough to discern a threefold typology of blood-symbolism employed by the Israelites in a religious setting.

First, there is the sign which brought deliverance from death. Before leaving Egypt the Israelites smeared their doorposts with the blood of a lamb (Ex 12:7. 13. 22f). This sign delivered them from the destruction which afflicted the homes of the Egyptians. The blood of the paschal lamb saved the Israelites from losing their first-born. There were other ways, too, in which blood was closely associated with *life*. The Israelites understood life to be "in the blood" (Lev 17:11ff; see Dt 12:23). Since life was sacred, they regarded blood also as sacred. Yahweh was the God of life.

Hence blood, the seat of life, belonged to God alone. In the ancient Near and Middle East, the Israelites appear to have differed from all their neighbors *in linking blood with life, and hence with what was sacred and divine,* at least in the symbolism dealing with sacrifice. In its own way, modern science has more than vindicated the Old Testament conviction that life, the divine and sacred gift *par excellence,* is "in the blood." Oxygen, nutrients, hormones and other items essential for life are carried by our blood. Its complex structure enables us to endure wide variations of temperature and changes of diet. Every day around the world massive transfusions of blood save lives that are slipping away. Medical discoveries and practice have dramatically associated the miracle of life with the miracle of blood.

Besides expressing deliverance and life, blood was believed to cleanse the stains of human sin. On the Day of Atonement the high priest sprinkled blood as part of a ritual recalling God's willingness to purify the Israelites from their sins. Yahweh wished to remove human guilt, destroy sin and effect reconciliation with his people. The ceremony of sprinkling blood on the "mercy seat" symbolized the divine desire to wipe away the contamination of sin (Lev 16). Today, of course, we may not appreciate the practice of slaughtering bulls and goats to release and use their blood. But we should still be able to recognize the religious logic of the Israelites. Insofar as it was the element in which life resided, blood enjoyed a peculiarly divine and sacred character.

Hence it appropriately served and stood for the purification of sin and the restoration of loving relations between Yahweh and his people.

Third, blood sealed the covenant at Sinai (Ex 24:3–8). Even today some cultures and sub-cultures maintain this symbolism. Rituals involving blood bind together formerly hostile groups and bring new relationships of peace, friendship and love. In the desert, the Israelites solemnly accepted Yahweh's offer of a special relationship with them and used blood to represent this loving union with their God. The sacrificial blood was shared by the people and their God (represented by the altar).

Here then are three perspectives on blood recorded in the Old Testament: as a sign of deliverance and life, a ritual means of expiating human guilt, and a way of sealing and expressing a new relationship of friendship. Even in the advanced industrial culture of the late twentieth century this triple typology persists at least dimly. When a society lacks life, we call it anemic. Parents show alarm when their children suffer cuts. There is a danger that blood will be lost and dangerous infection will set in. The bloodstained seat of a car can speak very powerfully of a precious life being terminated by terrorists. Blood donors literally give new life to others. The point does not need to be labored. Both positive and negative associations of ideas link blood with deliverance from death to life. Admittedly we have become sadly used to the fact that noble people—the J. F. Kennedys, the Romeros, the Sadats—may dedicate themselves in heroic service only to be murdered and soon forgotten. So much bloodshed seems irrelevant for the purifying and healing of a contaminated world. Yet there always remains the hope that the love inherent in the true sacrifice of a Martin Luther King or an Oscar Romero will somehow make its impact, that in some way the deaths of these victims work to cleanse and atone for the sins of our society. Though it remains true that the call to give one's life for others has been introduced in a thousand evil causes, no abuse can rob Jesus' words of their truth: "Greater love has no man than this, that a man lay down his life for his friends" (Jn 15:13). Whether in fiction or in real life, there can be no more powerful way of symbolizing and enacting a relationship of love than by shedding one's blood for others. True love always makes people vulnerable. Sometimes it literally turns them into targets for killers.

## THE BLOOD OF JESUS

It takes no great imaginative leap to see how this triple typology is supremely realized in the case of Jesus' bloody crucifixion. As our paschal lamb (1 Cor 5:7; Jn 1:29. 36), he freely accepts death to deliver us from the power of sin and bring us life and freedom. To eat the flesh of the Son of Man and drink his blood is to receive eternal life (John 6:53–56). Secondly, the First Letter of John witnesses to "the blood of Jesus" which "cleanses us from all sin" (1:7; see Jn 1:29). Finally, the shedding of his blood effects a new covenant of love between God and the whole human race—"gathering into one the children of God who are scattered" (Jn 11:52). This death expresses the divine love toward us (Jn 3:16), a love which is supremely "fruitful" in bringing people to God (Jn 12:20–24).

These then are three perspectives which stand behind the Johannine witness to the blood and water which poured from the pierced side of Jesus. But we are dealing here with a symbolic reality. Something further needs to be added about the power and meaning of this symbol.

Symbols enter our imagination, affect our feelings and influence our behavior by making things present. Symbols are felt to be powerful and important even before we consciously perceive their possible meanings. Further, over and above those meanings which society generally associates with given symbols, different people will recognize and appreciate different meanings for themselves. Cultural and historical conditioning brings it about that the perception of symbols will vary from period to period and from place to place. In all cases, rational explanations will always fall short of the potential range of meanings expressed by given symbols. Particularly when we take up religious symbols (like the precious blood of Christ), which point to ultimate, transcendent realities, we can expect these symbols to prove inexhaustible.

Small but precious details in John's passion story suggest the richness of the symbol we are examining. For instance, Jesus shed his heart's blood before *and after* death. In a brutal act of aggression, a Roman soldier ran a spear through the side of the corpse on the cross. At once water and blood flowed from this final wound (Jn 19:34). The memory of this symbolic episode evokes the sense that in life, at death, and even beyond death, Jesus gave himself *totally,* just as his crucifixion and resurrection aimed to reconcile the entire universe with the Father. Further, the opened side of Jesus released grace into the world under the signs of blood and water. The dead victim offered life, cleansing and love to his crucifiers and to the sinful humanity they represented. I sketched above the Jewish understanding which links blood with all three gifts. Here we might catch the nuances better by associating life and love with the blood, and cleansing with the water, which flowed from the wounded side of Jesus.

In rereading the Litany of the Sacred Heart before writing these words, I was intrigued to find that it makes no explicit reference to the blood of Jesus, even though it contains such invocations as "Heart of Jesus, pierced with a lance." Does it need the addition, "Heart of Jesus, giver of your life's blood for us"? The blood which issued from Christ's wounded side and flowed down the body on the cross was blood which had passed through the heart of the Crucified.

As a symbolic reality, blood maintains its hold on the popular mind and feelings. We can still hear the message of John 19:34, Colossians 1:20 and other such New Testament passages: by shedding his blood on the cross Jesus brought peace and reconciliation to the whole world. At the same time, however, the symbol has its distasteful, even cruel aspect. Consummately, as a symbol touching the divine-human relationship, it exemplifies wonderfully well the "frightening and fascinating mystery" *(mysterium tremendum et fascinans)* that we encounter in God. To reflect on Jesus' blood is to think of something which concerns and evokes both desire and dread.

To conclude: As part of their total passion narratives the other Gospels include the story of the institution of the Eucharist, during which Jesus took a cup of wine and said, "This is my blood of the covenant, which is poured out for many" (Mk 14:24 and parallels). John's story of the Last Supper, however, includes no narrative of the institution. Rather it does something we do not find as such in the other three Gospels by referring to Jesus shedding his blood on the cross. Instead of the sacramental preparation and pledge on the eve of the crucifixion, we read in John of a final, bloody wounding after death. The reader finds there the fulfilment of that mysterious promise: "Out of his heart shall flow rivers of living water" (Jn 7:38).

## NOTES

1. Some texts of Luke allude to Jesus' sweat becoming "like" drops of blood in the Garden of Gethsemane (22:44). But the most reliable ancient authorities do not include this verse.

2. Jürgen Moltmann, *The Church in the Power of the Spirit* (SCM Press: London, 1977), p. 86.

3. *Ibid.*, pp. 88f.

4. Of course, one should remember that "Corpus Christi" is now officially the feast of the most holy body *and blood* of Christ.

# Epilogue

This little study of Johannine spirituality could well carry another title. In place of "Finding Jesus" we would do better to think of "Being Found by Jesus." In the Gospel Andrew tells his brother, "We have found the Messiah" (Jn 1:41), but we know that in the deepest sense it was the other way round.

My book has moved from the words of Jesus to the silence of his bleeding body on the cross. It began with Jesus the Questioner and ended with the extraordinary symbol of his wounded side.

While I was writing much of the text, I was visiting each Sunday an army barracks where the chapel board carried a sign: "With faith there are no questions. Without faith there are no answers." How wrong the first statement is! With faith the questions change and deepen, but never go away. The Jesus of John's Gospel directs his questions at believers and non-believers alike. It can be painful to hear those questions; it may be even more painful to let them range over our current social and political situation. "Will you visit me when I am sick, deprived and old? Will you feed me when I am hungry or will you continue to indulge in conspicuous over-consumption? Will you let fear and greed dominate your lives? Will you destroy yourselves through a desperate anxiety for national security?"

In a sense it all comes back to two symbols: a wounded heart on a cross and a cenotaph in Hiroshima where the following words are carved in stone: "Rest in peace, for the mistake will not be repeated." As we look at those two symbols, it ultimately reduces to that one question: "What are you looking for?"